Turn Your Hurts Into Harvests

KENNETH COPELAND

Harrison House
Tulsa, Oklahoma

Turn Your Hurts Into Harvests

ISBN 1-57562-236-X   KC-236-X   30-0058

07 06 05 04 03 02 01 00 99 98   10 9 8 7 6 5 4 3 2 1

All scripture is from the *King James Version.*

Reprinted 1998

Published by Harrison House, Inc.
P.O. Box 35035
Tulsa, Oklahoma 74153

Turn Your Hurts Into Harvests

What do you do when someone mistreats you?

I didn't ask what you *want* to do. I didn't ask what your automatic fleshly reaction is. I already know that.

Your natural, knee-jerk response is the same as mine. You want to strike back. You want to do something or say something that will even the score. If you can't manage that, you might settle for a few hours (or days or years) of feeling sorry for yourself. You might try to ease your wounded feelings by telling someone how wrongly you've been treated.

On a purely natural, human level, that's how we all want to react when someone does us wrong. But I want to tell you something today. If you're a born-again child of the living God, you have no business just reacting to things on a natural, human level.

God has called and equipped you to live on a higher level. He's given you the power to respond in a supernatural way when someone does you wrong. He's given you the power to respond in love.

"Oh, Brother Copeland, that's too hard. I don't want to do that!"

Yes, you do—and here's why. If you will train yourself to respond God's way, you can take mistreatment and transform it from the curse the devil intends it to be into a seed of tremendous blessing in your life.

When you learn to obey God in the face of persecution, you can literally get rich—in the areas of finances, favor and opportunity—off the very persecution the devil sent to keep you down.

Serious Business

Make no mistake, that *is* the devil's intention. He sends people across your path to offend you and mistreat you for the express purpose of stealing the Word of God—and the anointing that goes with it—out of your life. Mark 4:17 says, *"Persecution ariseth for the word's sake."*

The devil knows how powerful you are when you are anointed. He knows because he once was anointed himself. The Bible says before evil was found in him, he was the "anointed cherub." So it is his one ambition to trick you into cutting yourself off from that anointing.

That's why he sends bigots to insult you and thieves to steal from you. That's why, whenever he can, he goads people around you into being insensitive and unappreciative. He wants you to get offended and cut off your supernatural power supply.

Most believers don't realize it, but that's what offenses do. You can see that in Matthew 11:4-6. There, the disciples of John the Baptist came to Jesus and asked if He was truly the Anointed One. Jesus answered and said to them:

> **Go and show John again those things which ye do hear and see: The blind receive their sight, and the lame walk, the lepers are cleansed, and the deaf hear, the dead are raised up, and the poor have the gospel preached to them.** *And blessed is he, whosoever shall not be offended in me.*

We need to realize, my friend, that offenses are serious business. They are sent by the devil to rob us of the anointing and block the flow of the blessings of God. That fact alone should be enough to make us decide never, ever, to be offended again.

I know I've made that decision. I've determined that no matter how someone may insult my intelligence, my beliefs or even my race, I'm not willing to lose my anointing over it.

No matter how they treat me, or what they might call me, I will not take offense.

Now I realize someone may be reading this and thinking, *Yeah, that's easy for you to say! Nobody says and does the things to you like they do to me!*

That may be true. Although I am an Indian, and have had ample opportunity for offense where race is concerned, I know there are many people who have suffered much more mistreatment than I have. But I can say this: No matter what color you are, you are welcome in more churches than I am. I've had entire books written for the express purpose of criticizing me. How many books have they written about you?

I only bring those things to your attention because I want you to know that dealing with offenses isn't any easier for me than it is for anyone else. I've come up against some hard people and some hard situations in my life. So I know if God can see me through, He can do the same for you.

Rejoice!...No Kidding

Once we decide we will take a devil-sent opportunity for offense and turn it into a harvest of blessing, the first thing we need to know is what God wants us to do in that situation. If we're not supposed to strike back, if we're not supposed to get our feelings hurt and go off in a huff, what are we supposed to do? First Peter 4 answers that question:

Beloved, think it not strange concerning the fiery trial which is to try you, as though some strange thing happened unto you: But rejoice, inasmuch as ye are partakers of Christ's sufferings; that, when his glory shall be revealed, ye may be glad also with exceeding joy. If ye be reproached for the name of Christ, happy are ye; for the spirit of glory and of God resteth upon you... (verses 12-14).

God doesn't want us to cry and complain when someone does us wrong. He doesn't want us to sue them. He wants us to REJOICE!

I can just hear your old flesh groan: "Man, you have to be kidding! I'm supposed to rejoice when someone does me wrong? What do I have to rejoice about?"

Plenty!

According to Jesus, persecution sets you up for blessing. It opens you up for great rewards! Jesus made that very clear in Luke 6. He said: *"Blessed are ye, when men shall hate you, and when they shall separate you from their company, and shall reproach you, and cast out your name as evil, for the Son of man's sake. Rejoice ye in that day, and leap for joy: for, behold, your reward is great in heaven..."* (verses 22-23).

To get the full meaning of what Jesus was saying there, you have to realize what the word *blessed* means. It's not just a weak, religious sentiment. To be God-blessed means you're empowered by Almighty God Himself to prosper and succeed. It means you're empowered by the Holy Spirit to be exceedingly happy with life and joy in spite of any outside circumstances.

Think about that for a moment. When people mistreat you, they're actually giving you the opportunity to receive greater measures of power and success from the Spirit of God. They are opening the door for you to step up to a higher plane of heavenly reward!

Religion has taught us that we couldn't enjoy such heavenly rewards until after we die. But nothing could be further from the truth. God intends for us to make use of our heavenly rewards here on this earth where we need them!

You see, as believers, we each have a heavenly account that functions much like a natural bank account. The Apostle Paul refers to that account in his letter to his Philippian partners. He commended his partners for giving to him, not because he wanted gifts from them, but because he desired fruit that would abound to their account.

Paul's partners had made deposits in that heavenly account through their giving, so he was able to boldly say, *"My God shall supply all your need according to his riches in glory by Christ Jesus"* (Philippians 4:19).

Jesus also spoke of that heavenly account when He said:

> **Lay not up for yourselves treasures upon earth, where moth and rust doth corrupt, and where thieves break through and steal: But lay up for yourselves treasures in heaven, where neither moth nor rust doth corrupt, and where thieves do not break through nor steal: For where your treasure is, there will your heart be also (Matthew 6:19-21).**

If you've studied the Word under this ministry any length of time, I'm sure you already know how to lay up treasure in your heavenly account by giving financially into the work of God. You know about the spiritual law of seed, plant and harvest. You know that when you give to God of your material resources, He multiplies it and gives it back to you a hundredfold (Mark 10:30).

But let me ask you this: Did you know you can do the same thing with persecution? Did you know that you can plant it as a seed by obeying God, by leaping and rejoicing in it instead of taking offense?

Sure you can! And when you do, it will bring forth a harvest of blessing!

What's more, because persecution attacks your soul and the very anointing of God on your life—which is far more precious than anything money could buy—the value of the harvest it brings is absolutely priceless. The seed of persecution when planted according to the Word will be worth far more to you than any financial seed you could ever plant!

Now, I'll be honest. It's a tough seed to sow. You have to sow it out of commitment. It doesn't feel good to do it. But the harvest is worth the pain.

I know that not only from my own experience, but from watching the experience of others. One friend of mine, for instance, has refused to take offense at the bigotry directed against him because of the color of his skin. He has so succeeded in blessing and loving the white people who have persecuted him that now some black people are mad at him. "He doesn't even know he's black anymore!" they'll say.

But my friend doesn't take offense at them either. He just prays for them and goes right on gathering up his harvest. It's quite a harvest, too! That man has favor everywhere he goes. He's invited to places few people get to go. He's blessed financially beyond most people's wildest dreams.

The man is getting rich off racism!

It's Worth More As a Seed

Someone might say, "Well, that sounds good! I wonder if it would work like that for me?"

It will if you'll put it to work. Look back at that passage in Luke 6:27 where Jesus explains this principle and says, *"I say unto you which hear...."* In other words, this will work for anyone who will listen. All you have to do is hear it and do it.

Love your enemies, do good to them which hate you, Bless

them that curse you, and pray for them which despitefully use you. And unto him that smiteth thee on the one cheek offer also the other; and him that taketh away thy cloak forbid not to take thy coat also. Give to every man that asketh of thee; and of him that taketh away thy goods ask them not again.... But love ye your enemies, and do good, and lend, hoping for nothing again; and your reward shall be great, and ye shall be the children of the Highest: for he is kind unto the unthankful and to the evil. Be ye therefore merciful as your Father also is merciful. Judge not, and ye shall not be

judged: condemn not, and ye shall not be condemned: forgive, and ye shall be forgiven: Give, and it shall be given unto you; good measure, pressed down, and shaken together, and running over, shall men give into your bosom. For with the same measure that ye mete withal it shall be measured to you again (verses 27-30, 35-38).

For the most part, we've misunderstood what Jesus was saying there about turning the other cheek and giving to the guy who tries to steal from us. We thought He was saying we should just lie down and let people run over us. But that wasn't His point at all!

He was trying to teach us about this seed, plant, harvest principle. He was trying to show us how to get blessed. He was saying, "Don't sue the person who stole your shirt and try to get your shirt back. Give it to him. Then give him your coat too. Those things will be worth more to you as seeds than they would be if you kept them. If you'll sow them instead of fighting to keep them, the power of God will go to work on your behalf. He'll multiply that seed and bless you with a hundred times as much!" If you fight, you do it on your own. If you give, all of heaven will get in the situation with you.

I'll never forget the first time God was able to get the truth of that principle through to me. It was years ago when Gloria and I were on our way to preach a meeting in San Francisco. I was walking through the airport with a little Minolta camera hanging over my shoulder. Back then, that was the ministry camera and Gloria was the ministry photographer. So that camera was important to us.

I had walked around that airport for a while when suddenly I realized my camera was gone. Someone had stolen it right off my shoulder! To put it very mildly, I was irritated.

I started looking around the airport for the thief. I thought, *If I find you, you turkey, I am going to whip you good!*

But right in the middle of my upset, the Spirit of God interrupted my thinking. *If you take that attitude,* He said, *you'll lose that camera!*

"What are You talking about, Lord?" I answered. "I've already lost it!"

No, it isn't gone yet.

I'd learned from Brother Oral Roberts about the seed, plant, harvest principle, so I caught on to what the Lord was telling me in a flash. I said, "Lord, I see it!" Then I turned to Gloria and said, "Listen, let's agree on this. I'm giving that camera to whoever took it off my shoulder. I'm sowing it as a seed into that person's life and I'm praying that God will use it to get him saved. I'm believing that every time he touches that camera, the anointing of God will come on him and draw him to Jesus. Even if the police catch the thief with the camera in his hand, I will say, 'Don't charge that man with any crime. I have given him that camera.'"

Of course, Gloria agreed and we boarded the plane to San Francisco. After we got settled in our seats, I started talking to the Lord about the seed I'd planted. I said, "Lord, I know that camera had value and we need a camera in this ministry. But I don't want another Minolta. It's a good camera, but it doesn't have enough range to do what I need. What I want is a Nikon F."

This was back in the early '70s when just the body of a Nikon F was worth anywhere from $700 to $900. The two lenses I needed were worth about the same amount, so to buy the whole outfit, I might have to pay up to $1800. But I wasn't worried. I had my seed in the ground and I started getting excited. I started expecting the harvest.

What a Deal!

Can you see what happened to me? I could have been sitting there seething over that stolen camera. I could have been sitting there getting offended, cutting myself off from the anointing of God. But I wasn't! I had forgotten all about that thief. I was too busy being thrilled with the new camera God was giving me to worry about how the thief had done me wrong!

A few days later, Gloria and I were walking along the street in San Francisco when I spotted a Nikon F camera box sitting in the window of a small shop. I went in and asked the store clerk how much they wanted for it.

"We don't have a Nikon F," she answered.

"Yes, you do. It's right there in the window."

She reached over and got it, looked puzzled and carried it to a Japanese gentleman in the back of the store. "How much is this?" she asked him.

He threw up his hands and said something in Japanese that I didn't understand. So I just dug around in my pocket and found some traveler's checks. "Here," I said, "I have $250. Will you sell it to me for that?"

"OK!" said the Japanese man.

Of course I was excited about getting just the body of a Nikon F for that price. But before I had a chance to say anything about it, the store clerk dug around in a drawer, found a Nikon 50 mm lens and handed it to me along with the camera. Glory to God, my crop was coming up!

It wasn't finished yet, either. Just a few days later in another city, Gloria and I were walking along the street again and we stopped in a camera store. I looked up and noticed that way up high on the top of a display shelf there was a lens case for a Nikon 200 mm lens.

The same thing happened again. The store owner didn't know he had it, and didn't know what to charge for it. So he sold it to me for $100!

I don't mind telling you, by the time that deal was done, I was almost hoping someone would steal something from me. But then I realized, *Hey, I can give it—without someone having to steal it!* I liked that kind of harvest!

You'd like that kind of harvest too, wouldn't you?

Well, you can have it. Just start taking those opportunities for offense and planting them as seeds. Instead of crying over how badly you've been hurt, turn those hurts into harvests and start laughing at the devil. Take everything ugly he has ever thrown at you and sow it as a seed.

Begin now by praying: *Father, in the Name of Jesus, right now I sow as seed in the kingdom of God every hurt, every bad feeling, every theft, and every evil thing any person has ever done or said to me, my family or my ministry. I release every person who has ever hurt me and I forgive them now. I lift each one of them up to You and I pray for those people. I pray, Father, that they'll come into a greater knowledge of You. I pray that their spirit be saved on the Day of the Lord.*

Now I declare before You, My God in heaven, that I expect a reward. I believe Your Word and by faith I set my sickle to my harvest. I believe I receive a hundredfold return for every wrong deed done *to me, every unkind word spoken to me and every dime stolen from me. I expect to receive a blessing of equal benefit. I claim it. It's mine and I have it now in Jesus' mighty Name!*

Prayer for Salvation
and Baptism in the Holy Spirit

Heavenly Father, I come to You in the Name of Jesus. Your Word says, *"Whosoever shall call on the name of the Lord shall be saved"* (Acts 2:21). I am calling on You. I pray and ask Jesus to come into my heart and be Lord over my life according to Romans 10:9-10. *"If thou shalt confess with thy mouth the Lord Jesus, and shalt believe in thine heart that God hath raised him from the dead, thou shalt be saved."* I do that now. I confess that Jesus is Lord, and I believe in my heart that God raised Him from the dead.

I am now reborn! I am a Christian—a child of Almighty God! I am saved! You also said in Your Word, *"If ye then, being evil, know how to give good gifts unto your children: HOW MUCH MORE shall your heavenly Father give the Holy Spirit to them that ask him?"* (Luke 11:13). I'm also asking You to fill me with the Holy Spirit.

Holy Spirit, rise up within me as I praise God. I fully expect to speak with other tongues as You give me the utterance (Acts 2:4).

Begin to praise God for filling you with the Holy Spirit. Speak those words and syllables you receive—not in your own language, but the language given to you by the Holy Spirit. You have to use your own voice. God will not force you to speak. Worship and praise Him in your heavenly language—in other tongues.

Continue with the blessing God has given you and pray in tongues each day.

You are a born-again, Spirit-filled believer. You'll never be the same!

Find a good Word of God preaching church, and become a part of a church family who will love and care for you as you love and care for them.

We need to be hooked up to each other. It increases our strength in God. It's God's plan for us.

About the Author

Kenneth Copeland is co-founder and president of Kenneth Copeland Ministries in Fort Worth, Texas, and best-selling author of books that include *Managing God's Mutual Funds, How to Discipline Your Flesh* and *Honor—Walking in Honesty, Truth and Integrity.*

Now in his 31st year as minister of the gospel of Christ and teacher of God's Word, Kenneth is the recording artist of such award-winning albums as his Grammy nominated *Only the Redeemed, In His Presence, He Is Jehovah* and his most recently released *What a God You Are.* He also co-stars as the character Wichita Slim in the children's adventure videos *The Gunslinger, Covenant Rider* and the movie *The Treasure of Eagle Mountain,* and as Daniel Lyon in the Commander Kellie and the Superkids$_{SM}$ video *Armor of Light.*

With the help of offices and staff in the United States, Canada, England, Australia, South Africa and Ukraine, Kenneth is fulfilling his vision to boldly preach the uncompromised Word of God from the top of this world, to the bottom, and all the way around. His ministry reaches millions of people worldwide through daily and weekly TV broadcasts, magazines, audio and video teaching tapes, conventions and campaigns, and the World Wide Web.

Learn more about Kenneth Copeland Ministries by visiting our website at www.kcm.org.

Kenneth Copeland Ministries
Fort Worth, Texas 76192-0001

Kenneth Copeland Ministries
Locked Bag 2600
Mansfield Delivery Centre
QUEENSLAND 4122
AUSTRALIA

Kenneth Copeland Ministries
Post Office Box 15
BATH
BA1 1GD
England

Kenneth Copeland Ministries
Private Bag X 909
FONTAINEBLEAU 2032
REPUBLIC OF SOUTH AFRICA

Kenneth Copeland Ministries
Post Office Box 378
Surrey
BRITISH COLUMBIA
V3T 5B6
CANADA

UKRAINE
L'VIV 290000
Post Office Box 84
Kenneth Copeland Ministries
L'VIV 290000
UKRAINE